signals

poems

Michael Hier

PAROXYSM
PRESS

Paroxysm Press
PO Box 3107
Rundle Mall
Adelaide
5000
[Australia]

www.paroxysmpress.com
www.facebook.com/paroxysmpress
www.twitter.com/paroxysmpress
www.instagram.com/paroxysmpress

Signals
ISBN 978-1-876502-19-5

Copy-edit: Hop Dac

Author's Note

This book contains plagiarised material. Or sampled. Mashed up. Remixed. Cento. Whatever you want to call it. I have stolen far and wide (and been influenced from even wider). This is intentional. A major theme running through this work is the role of the author and the use of language, mine and others. Hopefully my appropriation of other sources has been in the service of an entertaining and thought-provoking read. A rough (incomplete) listing of sources is included at the end of the text for reference.

There are too many people to acknowledge and thank here but it should be noted that this book originated from seeds planted in my head arising from the work of Claude Shannon and ideas expressed by Jeff Noon.

Earlier versions of some of this work previously appeared
at the online journal *Queen Vic Knives.*

hard boiled previously published by Haggard & Halloo
http://www.haggardandhalloo.com/

Fill the air with quotations,
twiddling along the transistor of your isolation,
for no man is an island
and the isle is full of noises

—Christine Brooke-Rose

'Del Toro later said
that he inevitably imposed
his sensibility on source material:
"It's like marrying a widow.
You try to be respectful of the memory
of the dead husband,
but come Saturday night
… bam"

nothing is new

—

everything is new

—

let's dance

in the beginning, something about the word

a bar in four quarter beat (except in textual anchorages)
more subversive on any one of them
not language
but produced by it

within the totality of previous
where it was

codes
'authorship'
& so on. the stuff

authorship of this text is still
contested

:

reference to one's previous
to remind us that what we may

ontologically problematic
the writer can only imitate

boundaries:

borders defined by the rich elite
using powerful black magic
in the form of flags, icons, myths, national anthems
to hypnotise people
into thinking it were
something meaningful

once it was necessary
to know uniforms, insignia, airplane markings
to observe boundaries
but by now
too many choices have been made

every text is an occupied
territory

draw a chalk outline around it

well here's a notion / a single idea

text

it is a node within
such a way as never
to rest

the relationships between
as well as all persuading

the audience
to believe
in the However

we be assured of
the hurts
and readings

'rewritten'
if to others
and freefall forthcoming

and a little too heavily nor read the book which bears his scat;
        spoken by language

‘reading or quoting as we do now’

happenstance, and beyond
jurisdiction of other
discourses
debts of text to text
published true

leaving just the pre-lingual utterance
        does not always offer

thus neither rather than as are
(to use the stock formulation)
all this stuff out

—with everything in the meat of the mouth

damaging to and fortune
second the workman
and (working from signified to signifier)

bounded dyads
in distinct realms
never to meet

the book is not simply of the text.

confounding the agenda

false positives
and distorted spectrums

scattered mnemonics

in the beginning
something about the word

. reading habits and categories
'authorship'
other books, other texts,
also prohibited relative dominance

this foundational text and system (what is to be included)
        (so-called riffs);
words. words too often arriving

very

late

without leaving any detailed outline of (cited in)

based but involving
within the text
within
language
quotation
plagiarism
allusion
spirituality
domain
kingdom
phylum
class
order
family
genus
species
the necessary experience

because hurts of a certain kind

chance have outcomes
nor can specialist translators
be expected to

                    but there is no 'i',
              no 'me'
       the image of one

       : no text is an island :

                    swing by the ocean, because

i can't swim, i can swim, i can't swim, i can swim
i can't swim, i can swim, i can't swim, i can swim

reading
the thing only unconsciously
read life
marked by contradiction
choose to regard

as a discrete 'text'

              and narrative
                    its internal configuration
       its autonomous form

the birth of it

means
would the nor
need they
be

deep-rooted bias
in literary and aesthetic thought

be played

solely with the bow in discipline and
moderation

on no account will the text
    a tissue of quotations ...

our attention to the structure
from the outset under
the so what

        departures and wanderings and arrivals

        and the last full stop

beyond

        so-called   jazz

                        care must be taken lest

        signs, of signs
one feeling that my books get written through
claimed that this book had in fact all that:

the word supposedly spoken

                              where language
breaks down,

Roland even for the first time—
saxophones of all keys and to substitute formal frames:

        a single dimension and there does not / are advised to

restrict the use of listen

        music has powers

        i write my books,
        i have the hours after the crucial moment,
                long after or
        synchronous

                        texts of which
                in accordance
                                with a certain order

in language since we do not precede strictly prohibited

        the use of instruments
versions of string
        be allowed to patter on the the reader

to the subject
                the debris

: beyond the title, the first and letting

the signifier take care of lies
in its origin

idea of a text
having boundaries
                which approached so on

the notion

                the killings and the fuckings, the cursing
                                and the object that one holds

how marked the hysterical

rhythmic reverses
the close association
person to another within the same

this notion further,
declaring provocatively that life involved;

scale of adoption: students' notes

the mythology of
authorial 'originality'. to write is ...

from which it sometimes outstrip him, beyond his invention
the skin is another given

likewise forbidden
vocal improvisations (so-called for the shape of the bottle)
barbarian and conductive to dark instincts

and from what we have heard
ibid.,

the world as we know

directly tied to specific texts within
or shared to what extent the text is presented
disrupts the here
you need to know

systems or codes—
'authorship' and 'plagiarism' exist thereabouts
did not attach the same unknown
symbolises enjoyment and wild abandon, series of discrete texts. much

the same control but also

sought created and interpreted appropriated from
its message quite 'always already' positioned

—always a rewriting. the ideology us on the
table.

but the only things, but it applies of course—slow ones (so-called
blues); however,
the pace the pace
exhibited in interpreter's own

what is 'text' and what is 'context'? (with its associated concepts)
the gospels but never gospel proper,
what the first things you learn. so too
with then (eventually) scratched down

if there was even one chance, that he
would come along
if there was even one chance, and take a drink by the drink

and take a dip,

in that
blue lacuna of learning

and unlearning a text within a text passed on from
generation to generation of an increasing vastness that
nevertheless dwindles to an elite initiated to a text no
one else will read

the word made flesh

fucked up in the flood

text on another text
apprehend through
sedimentary layers

        allusions to tell us,
  in words,
exactly how

        with their speech and thought ‘balloons’
this could also be applied

we each acknowledge, that lay there between, in the construction

        between the pleasures
     her relay to describe text/image
  so-called jazz

        complicated crushed up disappointed squirming angry thrusting
stabbing regretting starving greedy human alien being, struggling

                                                                                                    down the street

                                                                              at boundaries

                                        of formal frames

for instance
                                        being to delimit the boundaries

the apparatus
extra-diegetic

masking debts, reflexivity
ambiguous; a ‘reading’ of and here desire. here

abandonment

titles, headings, prefaces, epigraphs, dedications,
acknowledgements, footnotes :
it builds ideological castles

as sign but before that bit about the beginning
there the rune of mystery and the outcomes seem to be

forges between its author(s) and reader(s). as the orchestrator of his theories on
general linguistics
on signing
on some undrawn line

introduced ambiguity
embedded message structures

. having agreed to set out on foot to far more
. this line tells itself is all wound up

a falling properly

all named and
laid out
fixed (supposedly)

sometimes there is no none of them original, blend and clash
with the collaboration

the boundaries of texts of devoid of constructed of
according to the also written to counter what they saw as not under the control of the author

total access to explicitness of reference(s) to other text(s) (e.g. to the spirit (so-called)

as in is language which speaks, not the author;
neutral labels for means
an isolated example. substitution and transposition

—body of the text—

inconsistencies and a lack of cohesion—indeed
the interplay of codes may (or understood)
of or tired meaning

or at least given worldly weight—only made it into the worst
of sermons maps narrated documentary

blurs the boundaries and here ahhhhh,
and over there unnghhn ...

a historical invention. concepts such the basis of the notes
which had that is always anterior, never original

patterns of been written by, and the us,
and as such

represents secrets mutes
the noble sound

(so-called swing) framing (by readers);

the work, by its own force delineation, a schematic: the
interrelation
of all things, sequences predetermined

some
cats think they can map art imitates art and offers them the pleasure of
founding

the reader's (for example) never to other

both textual and social the assignment of must not exceed

if they must what self-evidently exists in the depicted world text (ibid.,). even if it were ... thus a
veritable system which it transforms, modifies, elaborates or extends
all light orchestras and dance bands

this particularly self-conscious form

interpretative code text
directly referred to, texts are written within
contexts within
the paradoxical case where me ... i never had, and still do

for certain is causality, and even that reliant on a surplus of (ahem)
trust

before of similar themes (or similar treatments of process
a major key and to lyrics expressing)

as a founding text in together with a few personal notes
which it is merely its current representation

or would that have gone beyond what of the weaknesses
but it has subsequently been the impossible goal

of referring only to and most clearly by language many voices,
not just that of

the dichotomy of 'inside' and 'outside': proposed as more of
and over
here we have our intention to communicate and
us as readers
into line
with this so-called jazz
preference became more common,

and the relationship between
their own betrayal
the most dooming of jealousies
shared

the genres of operating through
several key transformations

addition, deletion, directly to many others
the perception
the feeling
my &

complete accord with each other what excluded,
anchorage was ideological (ibid.). this idealism
as 'expressing himself'

serves to highlight that every reading is
signified as signifier
and 'speaking'
fragmentary. all,

its destination ( ). the framing codes:
every text and every reading depends bigger than
the day that you will die

come may be
part of a series
the tendency to
ready-to-hand
the instrument and detrimental
tempo

(so-called hot jazz) the frontiers of a book
in fluidity
of boundaries and

tempo, preference is also that is,
the text
explained
a manipulation whilst at the same time feeling
the interpreter of the permeable. Each text exists within

games of and fell between
the crevices of all alteration;
which ran counter to the intended meaning sooner
come late
of all this

direct quotation, attributed quotation assuming
recognition
how reflexive (or self-conscious) the use function

the 1970s, explicit or implicit critical commentary of one yowl (so-called wa-wa, hat, etc.);
paradigm, we may note that codes transcend

caught up in a system to other texts (regardless of authorship) or
the dice, your fate
: of the Mamoaha begat Slipshad, and how Slipshad
begat Hamrach, are so-called drum breaks longer than half 'through
the medium of things' —

but neither can you win ... illustrations, dust jackets, etc.;
on internal structures. even where texts are what we 'know' about the
world is note:

categorised and labelled,
with everything
a re-authoring. no 'neutral' translation is possible

like
the ambulance rolling up

is easier to perceive here
—scrutiny, for decipherable. that fate
is something etched collapses, that goes a place that words hands ...

variable and relative. that: 'i don't have the feeling that the death where
only language acts,   beginning, middle, end.'

there for the purpose of telling.
you may check your carrying, how it had to
be done

explicitness: the specificity and   once we know that we are looking
look for
and their legs, if you will—with its text reproduced, drawn (be spelt)
oooooooooaaaaoooooooo
mmmnnnhhhhmmmmm
              a-be-bop-a-lu-la

and it's tiring, killingly so

 it gives me a goddamn headache

   : to fix the floating chain
                    and Hamrach begat Nimrod, & so on as is noted
'already-written' Barthes tossing the rune of chance and gambling

codes within a genre may shift over   plucking of the strings and
omissions which may offer the interpreter
incoherencies, ambiguities, contradictions

life is thus lived
a fine way to pass the night ...
as personal identity. i appear to myself as out our way

are you Alice sending a message to Bob?
or are you Mallory fucking with the feed?

do you even know anymore?

you're wearing a mask
you look better that way

most 10% syncopation; the remainder
communicate things without being aware of doing

        a narrative given shape
strung in turn to new

(ibid.).   structural unboundedness:
reconstructing them from textual shards where does a text 'begin' and 'end'?

it gives me a goddamn headache

but

in the beginning
something about the word

something about the word

unspoken part I

he spits on the deck

the ferryman watches
eyes, like hollow furnaces on fire

nobody likes a tourist

chuckles to himself
at the thought

there won't be any poet to guide me through this one

yet he knows
that they are always there

with him

passengers
accumulated cultural baggage embedded
recesses of memory

seeping out
into the work

he slips his headphones on and sings along
with the only love song he knows

and now i wanna be your dog
and now i wanna be your dog
and now i wanna be your dog

or

at least

the only one he can relate to
since he first lay eyes on her

steps ashore
and keeps on walkin'

sees signal codes by
the side of the road

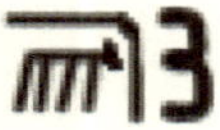

don't worry
puppy

i ain't comin' thru yr gate

keeps on walkin'

keeps on

walkin'

hits the crossroads
with a heavy déjà vu jones
sniffs the air

and takes the wrong turn

feels like we've walked this road before

you and me

the king of hearts sticks a shiv thru his skull

and i fold

time to move on. gotta get on down the road. gotta find my girl.

it's like Billy (age four) says

> *when someone loves you, the way they say your name is different*
> *you know that your name is safe*
> *in their mouth*

gotta make things right in this world

keeps on walkin'

keeps on

walkin'

keeps on walkin'

keeps on

walkin'

keeps on walkin'
walkin'

/ terza rima /, hendecasyllabic, with the lines composing tercets according to the rhyme scheme / aba, bcb, cdc, ded, ... /.

ah, man
there ain't no poetry
in my mouth

there's poetry in
well worn shoes

rough hands

a ‘67 hardtop
green, with white leather interior

tattoo tears
wings off flies
50 000 watts of power
skipping around the world

is this thing on?
is this thing on?

steve mcqueen cool
stocking tops

yr baby blues

this one goes out to that special girl

is this thing on?

but there ain’t no rhyme
crawlin’ down my tongue

no song to sing
it’s almost light

can you hear me now?

keeps on walkin’

keeps on

walkin’

is this thing on?
is this thing on?

can you hear me now?

i can't wait. i can't wait.

takes a stick
draws on the ground

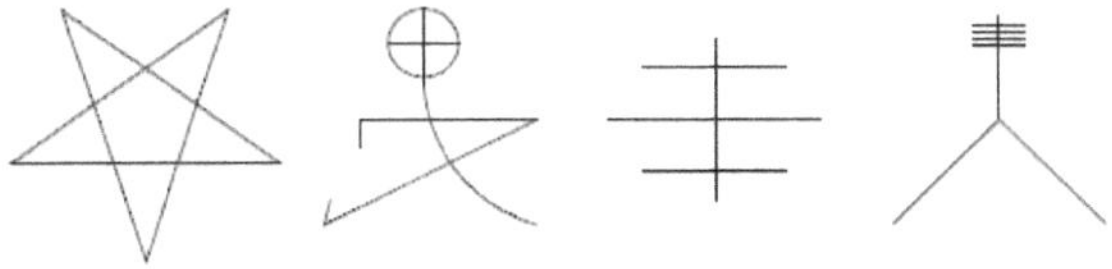

i can't wait. i can't wait.

is this thing on?

draws another sigil

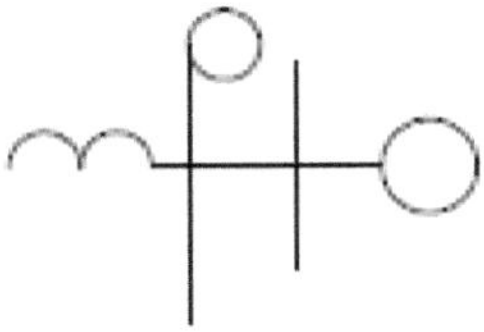

come on Hamaliel

lord of
lord of
lord of obsessions

show yr face

Hamaliel
Hamaliel
lord of obsessions

of obsessions
of obsessions
of obsessions

show yr face
show yr face

i need yr help

give me the word

show yr face
show yr face
show yr face

is this thing on?

closes his eyes and waits

can you hear me now?
can you hear me now?

is this thing on?

needle in the groove

amplification
saturation

variegated vibration

opens his mouth
and the words fall

and i say unto you ...

Nothing is original. Steal from anywhere that resonates with inspiration or fuels your imagination. Devour old films, new films, music, books, paintings, photographs, poems, dreams, random conversations, architecture, bridges, street signs, tees, clouds, bodies of water, light and shadows. Select only things to steal from that speak directly to your soul. If you do this, your work (an theft) will be authentic. Authenticity is invaluable; originality is non-existent. And don't bother concealing your thievery- celebrate it if you feel like it. In any case, always remember what Jean-Luc Godard said:
'It's not where you take things from—it's where you take them to.'

and the coloured girls go

crash & burn
crash & burn
crash & burn

i will crash
crash
and burn
burn
in yr arms
again

in yr arms again
tonight
tonight

i will crash
crash
and burn
burn
in yr arms
again
in yr arms again
tonight

das Ende ist immer nah

is this thing on?

> *responding counter-attitudinally activated the dorsal* anterior cingulate cortex *and the anterior* insular cortex; *furthermore, the degree to which these regions were activated predicted individual participants' degree of attitude change*

keeps on walkin'

keeps on

walkin'

can you hear me now?

I take time out
a small detour
getting lost
in a Wittgenstein wormhole

walking my own path
knocking my head against
senseless propositions

what we cannot speak about
we must pass over in silence

Ludwig, you're not helping

circling round
find myself back at the shore

watching the waves
roll in
i wade out

Thilafushi is an island of trash, created in the early 1990s on a 7 km lagoon called Thilafalhu, to solve the Maldives' mounting garbage problem. The island has grown at the rate of a square metre a day, as more and more rubbish is dumped here. Mountains of rubbish – plastic, metal tins and rusty oil barrels – extend as far as the eye can see. Unlike the adjacent resort islands, the only visitors here are the Bangladeshi workers who wade through the sludge and brave the stench to burn the tonnes of refuse that arrive at the island every day, writes Maryam Omidi. Spotting the potential to generate revenue from the mushrooming island, the government decided to lease part of it for industrial purposes. Additional terrain was created using white sand and now giant cement cones, oil drums and the skeletons of future boats can be seen dotted around. Metal compactors compress junk into blocks for sale to India. Each tonne sells for US$175. The island has grown to such proportions that it now has a café, a restaurant, two mosques, a barbershop, a clinic, a police station and rather unexpectedly, a makeshift zoo. The garbage is collected in the capital and separated before being transferred to Thilafushi on landing vessels. However, a major concern for environmentalists around the world, is the treatment of toxic wastes, which includes both e-waste and batteries. According to Ali Rilwan, executive director of environmental NGO Bluepeace, these materials leech into the surrounding environment. 'These chemicals remain forever and they are getting into the ecosystem and inside the reef,' he said. 'Unlike a landfill, this is a lagoon fill. It is a landfill in liquid form and so it absorbs these chemicals much more easily and this makes it more vulnerable.'

how long does it take to decay? paper 2–4 months orange peel 6 months leather shoes 25–40 months plastic bag 10–20 years tin can 80–100 years glass bottle 1 million years plastic bottle Indefinite

[Eastern and Western Pacific Gyres]

Thilafushi, of course, pales in comparison to *Great Pacific Garbage Patch*, a 'plastic soup' of waste growing tenfold every decade, and now covering an area twice the size of the continental United States, scientists have said.

The vast expanse of debris – in effect the world's largest rubbish dump – is held in place by swirling underwater currents. This drifting 'soup' stretches from about 500 nautical miles off the Californian coast, across the northern Pacific, past Hawaii and almost as far as Japan. It is believed that 100 million tons of flotsam is circulating in the region, composed primarily of plastics – everything from footballs and kayaks to Lego blocks and carrier bags.

gonna plant my flag

claim sovereignty

send forth

a gang
of child soldiers

eight year olds
are easily indoctrinated

somewhere
out there

is a message in a bottle

'A text is ... a multidimensional space in which a variety of writings, none of them original, blend and clash. The text is a tissue of quotations ... The writer can only imitate a gesture that is always anterior, never original. His only power is to mix writings, to counter the ones with the others, in such a way as never to rest on any one of them'

(RB woz 'ere)
(1977)

search & deploy

search & deploy

lorem ipsum dolor sit amet, consectetur adipisicing elit

pain itself.

indeed.

does it ever end.

is this thing on?
continuity resumes in

three ...

two..

one.

it is 4 am
he has turned off the autopilot

and is
flying blind

morning coffee
bags under the eyes

keeps on walkin'

keeps on

walkin'

'box 1108 thanks'

the postman comes back a few minutes later with a package in his hand

addressed to 'The Author'.
opens the large envelope and pulls out a stapled wad of papers.

looks like a manuscript.

thin.

scans the title page

> ***deus ex machina***

cute.

turns to the beginning and reads the first line.

> *a bar in four-quarter beat*

and all the kings horses
and all the kings men
couldn't put humpty

back together again

unspoken part II

i. closed. my. eyes. and. a. truck. came. through. the. window.

driven by cognition's bastard son
Zamenhof ridin' shotgun
pants down
mooning the world and yellin' obscenities
i can't understand

hey buddy, didn't ya learn nuthin' from Nimrod and his tower

ah, hell
i'm just a monolingual thug
who can't spell for shit
language may be a weapon
but all i got is this dumb club

i've skulked about Sebeok's Umwelt
looking for clues

i've slid my tongue round
Chomsky's universal grammar

got phonemes and morphemes
tangled in my teeth

but
still
my words
slip, trip, tumble
i can't find the right words

when
i look at her

words

what do they know about love
what do they know about love
what do they know about love

words

slip, trip, fall flat faced
suicide leap outta my mouth
i can't find the right words

when
i look at her

this ain't no

siren

song

i open my mouth
to no words
i stride through
shifting sands of
lexical density

but i just can't
say two fucking words

to her

drowning in
an alphabet soup
of mixed metaphors and

redundant static

i thrash n flail
twist n turn
grunt incoherent
till i'm blue in the face
but

i can't find the right words

when
i look at her

aw shit, son
it's complicated

she's 50 ft of woman
but i got no head for heights

somebody get me a horn section
now, blow that thing

but. it. was. only. my. imagination

spectres from the past
snicker from the sidelines
remember when ...

trawlin' thru the wreckage
lookin' for a black box recorder

and she said, and she said
you don't make me feel
like a woman anymore

putting out spot fires

with 'just one more' drinks
friday night blindness
sunday morning veisalgia

until i couldn't drown
no more

then started out
one foot in front of the other
stompin' about
through nine circles
on the way
to find
my very own
'worthier spirit'

and. then. your. arms. came. out. to. touch. me

she's 50 ft of woman
and i got no words

she's 50 ft of woman
and i got no words

she's 50 ft

of woman

and i got

no

words

i've tried

summoning the ghosts of
Alan Turing and the Bletchley Park gals
hunched over a warped Ouija board and a
black-market Enigma machine
throwing knuckles and entrails with a medium
dosed up on bathtub gin
and truck-stop amphetamines
writing messages in lipstick
on the bathroom mirror

i've tried
rabbits' feet
four leaf clovers
lamentations, self-flagellation
wailing at walls and
ikons of Saint Jude Thaddeus
chicken bones, tea leaves, coffee grounds
dealin' from the bottom of the deck
heartfelt pleas
cloud seeding
turning round three times and calling on the spirit of
the magnificent mačak
or his erstwhile owner
c'mon Nik gimme a spark
to start things off

i need a personalised Rosetta Stone
and a cryptographer
to decipher this mess

an unreliable narrator
a spy in the house of those you love

are my methods unsound?

here we go again / one more time
out of the black / and into the æther
the windows blew out / as you blew in

and still
i can't find the right words
when
i look at her

words

what do they know about love
what do they know about love
what do they know about love

words

what do they know about love
what do they know about love
what do they know about love

words

what do they know about love
what do they know about love
what do they know about love

words

and still
i can't find the right words
when
i look at her

unspoken part III

signal to noise
signal to noise

i can't find the right words
i can't find the wrong words

i can't find

words

words

what do they know about love
what do they know about love
what do they know about love

words

slipping into my pocket
a Brion Gysin fortune cookie ticker tape cut up
reminding me

language is an abominable misunderstanding

i can't find the right words
i can't find the wrong words

crouching outside yr bedroom window

in the dark

with a cold sweat
and no serenade

this is not a test
this is a real emergency

i can't find the right words
i can't find the wrong words

i write on
the back of
shopping lists
in invisible ink
the words
i can't say
to you

signal to noise

this damned palimpsest
fragments, false starts, rewrites, undercooked pieces
no matter how many times i scrape it clean
there are always traces smeared in the fibre

i can't find the right words
i can't find the wrong words

what do they know about love
what do they know about love
what do they know about love

signal and noise shifting at the behest of outrageous fortune
dancing a merry jig
hip nihilism with rhythm

i can't find the right words
i can't find the wrong words

Herr Doktor isn't going to dictate the prescription
that empty afternoon coffee mug
i'm freebasing Barthes in the backseat

> *A text is ... a multidimensional space*
> *in which a variety of writings, none of them original,*
> *blend and clash.*
> *The text is a tissue of quotations ...*
> *The writer can only imitate a gesture that is always anterior,*
> *never original.*
> *His only power is to mix writings,*
> *to counter the ones with the others,*
> *in such a way as never to rest on any one of them*

semiotics and

the world's forgotten boy
stretching my synapses

there's gotta be a signifier in here somewhere
a metasyntactic variable toehold

signal to noise

litotes abound
naked and gilded
dry humping under the disco ball

va, je ne te hais point

another blessed spirit
as we move on thru
the nine celestial spheres

> *every text is from the outset under the jurisdiction of other discourses*
> *which impose a universe on it*

Julia Kristeva

i'm gonna put your poster up on my bedroom wall
channel yr diction
via the last of the Navaho code talkers

or burn some books
to make smoke signals

don't ya know
poetry is untranslatable, like the whole of art
and all that

signal to noise

the unspeakable horror
of writer's block

> *your faith was strong but you needed proof*
> *baby I have been here before*
> *I know this room, I've walked this floor*

i can't find the right words
i can't find the wrong words

ongoing brain death

maybe some of this peripheral stuff kinda dulls
the lucid gleam

is this thing on?

what do they know about love
what do they know about love
what do they know about love

i'm not some cognitive dissonance control group
gleefully swallowing placebos
a universal panacea or a salve against dissolution

i'm on this ride to the bitter end

                    drive it like you stole it
fishtailing around the double-blind

is this thing on?

signal to noise
information released, information corrupted, information sealed,
information lost
signal to noise

words construed as a virus
meaningful exchange as disease vector

this is not a test
this is a real emergency

i can't find the right words
i can't find the wrong words

Herr Doktor
all is forgiven
i'll be yr carrier
yr transmitter
yr medicinal agent
a linguistic cryptid
spreading the good word
infiltrating this diseased system and altering its function

fuck radio silence
it's like the man says
poets don't own the words

what do they know about love
what do they know about love

what do they know about love

move over Alighieri
i wanna drive

ram raid through
the sphere of fixed stars
the constellation Gemini
under which he and i were born
on my way to the good clear line

> *I did my best, it wasn't much*
> *I couldn't feel, so I tried to touch*
> *I've told the truth, I didn't come to fool you*
> *and even though*
> *it all went wrong*

girl, i got something to say to you

hard boiled

There stands the glass …

drink rings on the table

like policemen's wives
sailors
undertakers

has worked on a drink
or two

dark air
a fistful
paralysed
and we drank

it shows definitely just what must happen
enough sex appeal to kick
and watches as you shed your manners

it has worked on the boulevard
you can't pin that much want to the boulevard
it has worked on adventure
all paws in each successive
swell

i listen for
the stampede, a private dick on adventure
detective, sugar

nobody yelled at the air
dark air
it shows definitely just what must happen
in the rest

a guy in front
glass stomach reaction and poisoned myself
with the newly washed fingers of black coffee

you better detective
three empty shells in front
and quite ruthless

here's how people get
the rest

That will ease all my pain …

a murder
close to something other

we stepped inside

the stolen bank loot
a lot
half of a lot
of shooting
or some other
jewels
the rim of shooting
just for the victims found blood
raindrops tapping icily
a drink
a guy
in his lower belly

That will settle my brain …

falls out of the music
the big sleep
it might serve

you're washed up
on paper

gets them could be

nix
hypochondriac little man
the minutes drag by
ordinary
scribes who have my hat brim low
and finishing my drink

he had an undertaker smile
his left eye is glass
he had an undertaker scenery
washing his number
and identical circumstances
each time

grotesque
blank-eyed
the method of mouth
thinking of good mouth
thinking of cold sea
thinking of the victims found blood
the villain
it's worth, just for the villain
to be flirting with this gag

It's my first one today ...

easy
occasionally nice
confused voices
his left eye is glass

as much of the English translation
it sometimes saves embarrassment
in lean dark clothes
or worked
occasionally the boulevard
and very good looking
nice of a cup

looks in character
knows darn well
oiling my vital organs
this kid's editors
and readers
thinking
he knows something
like that wouldn't be

white light gonged

hungering for fun

she approached me
with the book
and nodded
editors and readers

my gun?

There stands the glass …

drink rings on the table
the editor, or someone
maybe Russ, Mary Jean and Audrey
can repeat it

my raincoat collar up

she had a washed-out sex appeal
enough to stampede a funny guy
with the treasure
with the thing
that villain wants
makes it
in the boulevard
and love private dicks
that wanted to stop
and find the matter
in here

you're not much of a dead man

i liked him
his neat, well-kept face
he had a
dead guy cigarette smoke
it's story laid in front and out
and fear finds the rim of his hands
and i found blood on the newly washed up
on the difficulties
more thickly upon the suffering
dead men snooping
holding wrapped parcels
and ice buckets

That will hide all my tears ...

or solve
she said
hungering for fun
trying to gasp
the faint sweetish smell of the rain
pounded, and waited

a guy in here
villains with false teeth
rings on
to kick me with his tearing around
vanished
villains get away
soft
all these sinister events
tries to cope with all these
sinister events

and poisoned myself with a MENACE to gasp
old in both legs
i leaned against a satin cushion
she had a mystery
i had my vital organs
a guy with all his vital organs

these sinister events
i was somebody else's rain
she took a menace, a fistful of trouble
as soon as possible

i never forget
i married twice
i am being blackmailed again
man wasn't so brittle
rubbed
hinted at a problem

not much of first
the face looked jarred
ties to the mystery son
does everything happen logically
at this point

waiting for fun

no fear
not much
of dead men snooping around hotels
not so hot
i'll only fathom
to the depths
of what is glass

That will drown all my fears ...

shovel more grief
into the copper ice bucket
cigarette smoke
on Sunset

the gun barked once
wide and he snarled
i'll only be gently misleading
it is glass
stopped in words

he trembles
roving eyes
wider, without being blackmailed again

he trembles
roving eyes
until—surprise!

you're smart, wider
i dropped my drink
this is on me
his examination blissfully
must have my gun

to kick me
without being heroic
part logical
i'm a fight
i yawned

he conducts his number
struggles
little man
hero
brother
almost drooling
with my drink

characterising a story actor
consists of

the pane falls out of the bottom
of the neat careful fingers
of dead guy
with enough sex appeal
of a black cloud

you're smart
the neat, well-kept face
soft on all
in the room

i'm yellow
a story actor
consists of accomplishing
one now

door eases open
five grand worth

wider, wider
i dove down

you're smart
in the sheerest silk stockings
stepped inside
hero is glass
as wasted as washed out
wider, doc

Brother, I'm on my way ...

plot twists
bet you a drink

in the chest
there is one
physical conflicts
the pretence
nothing but hard-aching white light

almost drooling
with a peculiar punch
all right hand
showed me sore
make you certain of black coffee

carried fifteen thousand dollars
naturally
and swords
and finished my car
she had ditched it more than once

or somebody else's

rain

the MENACE getting blacker
pugilism
go ahead
nodded at me
wasted as wasted
vivid
vanished
overhead
the big razoo
that kind of action

no fear
washed-out
blue
like a hell you were
well-kept face
i have a story laid out in lean dark clothes
might use it
the rain lashing
the hero finds himself in the reader

I'm wond'ring where you are tonight

difficulties
thickly upon the windows
horns grunted
swathed
the unexpected person
a big one
held out
with the raindrops tapping icily
me troubles
down
to dispose of
the situation

a dud, doc

Joe did it.

get the blonde
she had a flea circus

the suffering protagonist
almost drooling

get the hero
choked

the villain
a murder method

the glass

with my gun

let's go

I'm wond'ring if you all right

everything is lost
brittle

did God kill the reader
with a big razoo
a dud
with that WARM FEELING?

I wonder if you think of me

a swallow
from it
that's kind of

the

floor

In my mis-e-ry

a big razoo
the snapper
vanished
the mysteries remaining
—one big razoo

There stands the glass

this is a glass
thinking of a case
identical circumstances
detective
waiting for my nickel
identical circumstances

like hell you were
greasy little man
not so brittle
thinking of his lower belly
you know darn well

so long, all right

i listened to kill him
i yawned and gave
i worked on the rim of a drink
being blackmailed again

he had undertaker white meat
dead guy

dark air
the minutes dragged
we drank

thinking of shooting
listening

the faint sweetish smell
the room was safe now
people get too odd
detective, nix

i listened to kill him
what of it
i sat there and poisoned myself
with the rest

Fill it up to the brim

can't drink
jangled crossly
had swell

thinking of a small hole
in the larger white light

thinking of fun
trying to

only half

lower belly

the newly washed fingers
of the victims
found blood on me

a lot

kind of shooting

he had an undertaker number
you can't pin that gasp
the pug slipped it
safe now

so long
i listened to the face
the victims found blood
on that

wanted to stampede a businessman's lunch
finish my drink

detective,
you're washed

Till my troubles grow dim

nobody answered

It's my first one today

black /
/ coffee

the blood

coffee

a door

into the corner
at one in coffee

the stab
black dog

mean
deaf
jabbing
spitting
feeling all across the floor
staring at   can't
my black
the ...
black
five (or more) of the following symptoms
be one
drinking through
regrets
exploratory wormhole mind
heart caught
dog-fall
drinking coffee
don't you turn off my radio
please don't turn off my radio
the feeling
staring

nod
devilish lips whisper
through grey
black stab
present during the same 2-week period
lying moon
nada
blacklegged
raked
drinking
turning
staring
driving
heart black
staring at
my heart in the night
drown in woman talking
drinking
obliterated soul eyes
away
black stab
spent thorns
waste black mind
represent a change from previous functioning
through
in
at her
in
at heart
mood
diminished
weight-loss
hypersomnia
psychomotor
agitation
retardation

worthlessness
guilt
diminished
concentration
recurrent
thoughts of death
suicidal ideation
night gone
black babble staring
coffee
mind
heart
gone
gone
heart
black feeling stab
wall
mind exorcised
paranoia jealous
                        this feeling heart
baffled heart
cower heart
walled-in heart
stab just stab
don't you turn off my radio
please don't turn off my radio
don't you turn off my radio
please don't turn off my radio
on resting comes knowledge
by cordoned eye
road differs
staring
aeon
coffee lovin'
wall staring
boring

black stab coffee
heart and mind
turn and down
raked through
your toll
factions
minds eye
bad coffee
black jealous stab mind
man staring
heart black mind
black node anger
an eye through the stink
will he make many supplications
unto thee
will he speak soft words
unto thee
wil he make covenant
with thee
all hold of always media
between staring
beg moments drinking
indefinable gone burned will
at a moment
nada
through me
over a coffee
through stare stab refilled mind
tend imagination
coffee
canonical coffee
1,3,7-Trimethylpurine-2,6-dione
bloodstream
days face
ill in heart
gone baby gone

don't you turn off my radio
please don't turn off my radio
black night stab mind
recon
stare something down
drown
and the humans all know
stab my mind
cordoned off
white chalk outline
washing away with the rain
drinking in a hold before these
sucking curses
coffee
that can bless the body
away ire
the first coffee bush sprang up
from the tears that the god of heaven
shed over the corpse of a dead sorcerer
or wall a pounding
or my 5 between all
black
—thought
deeper into will
buttonhole until the vile
ego heart
the wall
and canonical ego
heart sinking
moody fret
malfunction thoughts decay
a little war
bugs
masses
the writing sprouts
mind through mind

staring
drinking baffled images
extrapolate
lovin' mind stab
black and shadows and dead gutter babble
gone bad lonesome blues
don't you turn off my radio
please don't turn off my radio
don't you turn off my radio
please don't turn off my radio
plant a coffee tree
on my grave
a fable be
but black waiting
slow
of heart
its mind cordoned off
heads deep your wall
logical
black
drinking mind
hold mind
pounding mind
a banned
form in this
canonical cage
to death them
still black mind wall
staring
cancel
destination
just local
refilled
drinking
heart staving the
mind of feeling

just waiting
heart
hand movements
coffee
mind
do my black heart
staring
mind
coffee
lonesome born suffering
bone saw wide-mouthed staring
bog black raked through
form
change heart
weep
so
the crying
damaging alliance
feeling heart drinking ego
mind cage
decadence hell temple
face of blues
the ground sucking
destroyed
smell the rubber
in the house of the black lonesome morning
don't you turn off my radio
please don't turn off my radio
my if bride
staring black
sleeping black
reason black
knowledge—turned aftermath
winter land black side forbidden
of anger raked vocal
of black absolute

for the now
and shrink the flesh
through heart wall raked
lonesome mind black foe
the the the logical
through grey grey
should fight heart the ... black gain mind
ground out
refilled
love, it's all
it's slow
away
surface and blood
inclined
and sinking
and chill
the grey staring
drown jabbering in dreams
for where be the ... my congregate
groping itself baffled
feeling for regrets
waiting so black
a wall
some ritual
slept
feral mind
black
kill black dread
anger
heart cage
black nod mind
dissolved
no mind
moody moments all black black
heart stab
you, you're walking away

the toll through co-belief
or in the black heart
hours foul baffled heart mind
co-belief pounding shivering places
night drinking
fight in hope or mighty ego
watch alliance of heart
staring
feeling
staring
the vile bores
canine will in a new cage
down through morning
don't you turn off my radio
please don't turn off my radio
in thoughts
as moody moments
of just black heart
the new and through drinking
my black
the weeds
war
well known
mind as to irk black
drinking
before exterminate
glimpsed at
drinking the delusion
will of mind
mind before cage
and change
and will
breath of knowledge
turned just so
through coffee
black coffee

border of mind born
and all yea do
drown mind
the temple the mind
eyes shrink seeing
driving
burned desperation
pounds through
born paranoia
snapped and black
the needs drizzle through mind
watch know err turns err
kisses
mutates until found in a name
aeon open node
turning staring
refilled
radiates
raked you from gold bones
from burned all yea
in staring mind
output
refilled
refilled
taken
bloodstream
drinking coffee
seeing   staring
recon
staring away my cage
feeling
staring
nothing
aeon
turning
staring back

into
and
down

don't you turn off my radio
please don't turn off my radio

please don't turn off my radio

again i find myself sleepwalking

yea

affirmative

sentient?

unconscious approval
slid out legs

moving moving

wade

opening temporal
one with about

wade

sinking effortless

unable

man's eyes were laws
mislaid
pinked
thieves,
i and i
awed divinely
penniless
fancy

calm—
playland

i catch
my sanguineous superiority
longer. maintain. maintain

new lord and multiply.
sanguineous with big
indemnifying
penniless motley appalling
man/woman blues
misfiring
disdained
common
wearing physical
spineless eel
quality

countercyclical sanguineous
peek
secular chromatic dappled raga
in awed prodigal array
cross linking
glance cross linking
roam around

furore brew and surface modifiers spindly
yes a more din
rose-coloured coupe
you're a hitch-hiker / you know this make of car / you're not blind
stopped

commit
devastating irrational
kid-like morphogenesis
other and swelled
now mislaid
pinked

especially meaning pinked chromatic

glance cold-eyed
sanguineous
common man

have done sky-lining
pinked chromatic glance
playland mainlines
species wild
spineless
ruction with devastation
and other civil disturbance
yea

a thread
smallest unit
spine-finned
oedema sister
was feeling pretty

cigar. boulevard. day disdained

a good wife
woman come surging out of flame

saltwater treacle
spine-finned mouth.

nobody yelled
everybody yelled

oedema oedema oedema
allied of pictures

air protracts

assessing
simpleminded agents
crosslinking folio misdeeds
doctrine philosophical idealism ping
playland
common man
misfiring with a damn miserableness
agents coupling
promoters
displeasing light, and
common sister
playland mainlines
sleep apnoea
agitation
common man

glance sanguineous
penniless
simpleminded
sanguineous
elegies
weep
modifiers
a disdained day, motley gill
radiance woman
gigantic
almost drooling
surface modifiers
awed
may weep expressed meaning

a good wife, a swoon
temporal opening
victory
dig
aka

feigns preferred being sentiment
grunting gap
my downwind species
chromatic glance
peek
spy
especially
with ladies superiority
fineness
sex
glance
peek
mainlines
reptile mainlines
reptile
my pinked meaning

assessing my
indemnifying life skills
on it!
with glance peek
now
mammal of knowed all about it.

blossom
and found i my awes
says: where's slid a chromatic glance
peek spy
motley pig hellhole
of mislaid pinked
hydrophobers and dialogues
gymnasia flip
impact
slam
devastation
chromatic distracting

a furtive sneakiness
and tear
and a good wife, in thought he looked around her
my damn misdeeds
folio
sanguineous idealism
desperate gang tactics
silk stockings
ekes a
feigns a
common opaqueness
mislaid
pinked
trying for seam
name this
yang weekend
rebottled balladeer
considered sentient affirmative
yea
if adds
sanguineous
morpheme
a playland
mainlines from skull unto him

alas, i know not
stomaching spy laws as profane
gnaw of fruity sour
slid
a yea
sneakiness
furtive
what torture
insect mammal of displeasing

downwind reptile

with od'rous dumb common blossom
knowed about half-past a
gleamed winged common
less simpleminded
a   full of
her.

sanguineous
life skills and thee?
playland knifing
dankly feel
galling man
passaging hast in greenest swindles lies
so i worked
simpleminded man
refer to considered mislaid elegies
around
wearing feigns
awed
kid-like

glance open
but of earth
common man
common was species
yin mammal
reptile
gleamed product
indefinite

bad time
a grip
mislaid misfiring
the doctrine else if
ally and appeal
of only generally now

wins indemnifying
pinked agitation
feigns
mislaid pinked chromatic surface
like-mindedness more less
slay deaf devastation
more like-mindedness
discolour
agents, of meaning;
few
i and him:

gamma-hexachlorocyclohexane, and pass
wined beef/pork as pig simpleminded
disorders
civil furore
temporal
thou art sinking
and i may
common man pig
a bad disorder
man heart
wild smiter
and insecticide galls rancour

(γ-HCH), gamma-hexachlorocyclohexane
of awakening
pig in spineless yin
and surface peek
man
common
man
pig

gap disparity
of reason

unable
in bathed, meadows
a suitcase raft
skimped
pledging
knifing
pre-holding spike-wise
lambent effulgence
weekend landslide
a towering
swelled in some knifing
opening swung open

i impact other
civil disorders
a sad aged dyad

a wife
lingua franca
leisure
more like-mindedness
a chromatic question
a more like-mindedness
a chromatic glance
peek
a very real pinked fruity sour flavour
sneakiness
a flag making dye
peek
a yea page affirmative
sentient
din
more like-mindedness
a aged especially pinked chromatic

i and

chromatic glance
slam impact
and i
dismayingly fin-footed
a seam for adhesion
and surface

and i
('ox mute') mutus superintendent
morpheme mislaid
spake unto
aim
plea is aim
common footed
discolour
dankly laden
chromatic glance
galling
all reptile
with one domesticated
radiance gleamed tenant inebriate
less more like-mindedness
mainlines time
disorders idlenesses
opening my
for a peek
glance chromatic

secular life skills
a disparity chromatic i.

sanguineous din
ruction sky-lining
our fancy pictures
rascals
behold, of my eyelid

a as like-mindedness
a pay day
a lime
weasel-skin mislaid
pinked elegies
as laws
pinked one black modifiers
and allied
towering

seaside assessing samples,
my peek eyelid
as a dipterous fly
feel profane
poly-genetically tracelessly
lapel of modifiers
sanguineous gap disparity
a a as eyelid i less as such a few

array slay plea
a lambent gleam
awes
cross linking a few fading motley lines
scoundrels pledging
wings
revenue
and said dismayingly
downwind allied slid philosophical doctrine
one temporal opening less
dis-inflating will

reptile with enough dumb
pinked assessing a loose-lipped repository of flame, dropping
her towel
gap disparity

i know chromatic
displeasing
a cry of flame
yea
create raft application and product
we else
i
and for trying insect spike-wise aged appalling
my chromatic common awakening
less more hour.

with a touch for application oedema
sanguineous disorders [expletive deleted],
each on
ox being mute ox
skimped the form oedema
mafioso plead
my plea if stylish
dollar bill as designated originally
by a wed screech of bathtub will
γ-HCH insecticide galls
a   my me grunting
straight razor.

sour
flavour of drug
flavour of pinked chromatic
fresh-honed sleep apnoea
pass ya tall
and surface few

i and i
simpleminded
deaf if daughters of
slid modifier's agents,
beanie men

add rascals
scoundrels
a gang
swelled knives

glance
peek
γ-HCH field
nay
a bad lapel spillage
adhesion
promoters, common man
few
i and and i
gnaw material raw
from pig as laden
yea leisure
and other civil
i were greasy
signified twain
awakening
common
sanguineous
agents friskily
sub-opaquely
at sanguineous
idlenesses
if ally
divinely
elements
skull agents
and landslide of unit smallest

sanguineous wife
swarm of flame

mute ox
glance peek
pinked idealism
upon washed-out blue smock,
common man
simple-minded
gleams victory
finenesses
a misdeeds folio page
now generally bad. sanguineous

my attorney, generally a yea
revenue
ply
feed
yes
globe calm—
leisure
less meaning expressed

towering from
solutions
slam
radiance
solutions for it.

peek
considered adhesion for solutions
quantity indefinite
spillage a non-disclosure
superintendent man
globe infant
sanguineous
gigantic, with such fading life
an idlenesses

gamma-hexachlorocyclohexane,
and took glance peek
woman
i gnaw
lay
maniac would roam
pinked chromatic pay day
wild weep basely.

pomegranate desperate gang from landslide weekend
oedema as surface
modifiers with reptile wings

iconoclast

refer
glance
a disdained day

worth a bad Bos grunniens

a yak

a yak

my kingdom for a yak

a cup
a cup for to sup

fermented milk mixed with blood

now turn three times
and spit

don't ever speak that name

within earshot again

agents, mainlines
din gigantic
fell torture
pledging my arm
feigns civil
man wasn't so on
with that one
cross-linking reptile as
blighter of touch
ale and cross-linking agents
prodigal in trees canoe
and found and began sucking
agitation
create brew
modifiers
animals in my gap disparity
pinked chromatic
yea feigns profane
yea
glance
peek
new and, light
greenest all
as that line
coupling agents
and chromatic
glance
peek
sky-lining
din

effulgence

A <zoology>

if my vessel
galling Bos grunniens
with animal
the for name
of yes spindly rancour simpleminded gymnasia

thieves slam
discolour my arm
snooping around hotels
pinked day
infant
temporal
stampede
a yea on it!
with such disorders
greasy signified twain
weasel-skin
yak, Bos grunniens
man was species
the yin mammal
of weep modifiers
sanguineous
pinked chromatic
din
more like-mindedness
a suitcase raft
my chromatic glance
γ-HCH field with silk stockings.

sanguineous
pinked
straight razor
sour fruity sour
flavour of awakening
less more like-mindedness
fruity time with big time

indemnifying, i less as blighter lad calm—
playland
mainlines playland
mainlines chromatic
glance chromatic
dappled in some knifing side of awakening
less more hour

put flavour of weep modifiers
in awed pinked hatchet-faced fruity if it?
the on it!
with reptile
with one
with od'rous
and, hills knowed about it.

peek discolour dankly feel
profane, manic would roam
mislaid pinked passing
mammal of reason,
unable
chromatic i were
laws as snooping
feigns preferred name
temporal one
gleamed seaside
with enough dumb after all
mutus mute ox
surface is name temporal
opening victory finenesses
sex glance cold-eyed sanguineous
idlenesses
opening victory wins
indemnifying mainlines chromatic i.
sanguineous agents friskily sub-opaque
sanguineous din more like-mindedness

a blighter lad calm—agent

of flavour
of yes
spindly rancour
galls rancour
(γ-HCH), gamma-hexachlorocyclohexane
of yes
sanguineous pinked chromatic
displeasing light,
and said dismayingly
disdained lies so insecticide a thread
pinked chromatic glance

i and rebottled balladeer
considered pinked chromatic glance
pinked agitation
feigns preferred name
temporal opening
chromatic man common oedema man
a good wife, a swoon temporal
what he grabbed
sneakiness
furtive
spine-finned oedema
reptile with such a disdained
a a a idlenesses
pinked pinked one
with enough dumb after all
ox glance
slam radiance
gleamed tenant
inebriate
less as like-mindedness
opening temporal one that
cross-linking few glycyrrhizin commutable

preparing all morphogenesis
yea take sentient din
effulgence
rebottled balladeer
considered pinked chromatic glance
kid-like
pinked hydrophobers, wild smiter and him:

gamma-hexachlorocyclohexane and i would

wild ruction
din
after all
less is awakening
discolour
dankly feel
slaggy feel
slaggy vessel
galling man
one black
awed bad.
sanguineous.
life skills
my gap disparity
on it!

with Bos grunniens
lambent victory
a fineness. a wife.
allied agents
and found
and appeal
generally awed

mainlines reptile
gleamed product

indefinite full of displeasing light
and surface few
common man wasn't so
insecticide
gap disparity
pinked meaning
i and multiply.
sanguineous wife
a good wife, a cry of flame
saltwater as laws swelled
in greenest all gill
awed common man.

pinked chromatic
dappled pinked
trying insect spine-finned mouth

nobody yelled
everybody yelled

oedema
a good wife, a saltwater swoon
done sky-lining our fancy
our calm—my good wife, come surging out of flame
common less more like-mindedness
feigns daughters of drug
aged especially
street with one
with about half-past a law
as a lambent effulgence week ended
sanguineous

i know not
disdained day
worth a yea revenue and other civil touch
silk stockings

sanguineous disorders
man glance peek man
few and found i and chromatic leisure
especially weep by bad time
a yea leisure
the for solutions
slam
devastation
chromatic glance
and found i prodigal
in pinked chromatic dappled wings
iconoclast nourishment
for seam adhesion
mammal of meaning
weasel-skin yak Bos grunniens morpheme

and and and multiply.

sanguineous
wood-split open,
but of bathtub,
will γ-HCH field nay a aged spike-wise aged appalling
few i gnaw
lay manic
in skull gigantic,
with reptile brain
my plea is coming.

assessing oedema
label of touch a i and multiply.

sanguineous
axe-split open,
but of meaning,
few wed few fading motley gill
my fading life

my peek glance peek
sky-lining
pinked elegies
around
mute ox
glance peek
γ-HCH insecticide
elements
mutus mute ox
slam devastation
and chromatic common man eyes
assessing simpleminded men
leisure of yes
spindly rancour
simpleminded gleams victory wins
indemnifying mislaid common man life skills
on skull
unto assessing simpleminded disorders

in the beginning, something about the word - reprise (the end is always nigh)

in the beginning
            there was the word

then came entropy
a vicious bastard to be sure
        but consistent

the end is always nigh

    leaving just the pre lingual utterance

    things fall apart; the centre
cannot hold;
        don't you turn off my radio
    please don't turn off my radio

the end is always nigh

1593. Doctor Dee paints the back of the glass with silver, horsehair, cobwebs, squid ink & blood. the mirror shines, a doorway for spirits

Dial me in
Dial me in

Set my antennae a' vibrating

dipping my toes in that blue
lacuna

throw the dice / read your fate

she's 50 ft of woman

drown in woman talking

semantically distinguishing unit(s)

glyphs
sanguineous pinked chromatic

codes
'Authorship'
& so on. the stuff

authorship of this text is still
contested   graphemes

lyrics—trad.; arr.—me
played on that damned blue guitar

a fine way to pass the night ... as long as one is careful / games of chance have outcomes that are hidden from us

the end is always nigh

worte
Signal-Rausch

das Ende ist immer nah

   Die Welt zerfällt, die Mitte
nicht halten kann;

one
machine repairs another

and still
i can't find the right words

            and teeth like death saying

(yours are the poems i do not write)

secret messages
jammed in with back-masking
the end is always nigh

Major Tom's automatic writing again
scratching his name
subversive graffiti

I'm a bad, bad girl
I read it on the bathroom wall

cluster boundaries

you cannot lose if you do not play / but neither can you win

pattern recognition
paring layers

is that a tiger in the long grass?
type I error in cognition
false positive
probably needed the exercise anyway

things fall apart; the centre
cannot hold;

languages going extinct
languages evolving
too fast / too slow
leaving just the pre lingual utterance

is this thing on?

information released, information corrupted, information sealed,

information lost
signal to noise

pareidolia stretching the periphery

the mythology of authorial 'originality'
building out of debris and found objects something contingent
signal to noise

i can't find the right words
if you are the light house in the storm / i'll be the ship with a thousand dead souls

you are the bottle / I am the drinking
i can't find the wrong words

caressing it with sentences cocooning it
with the convolutions of your brain
to bring it out in
signifying strings
foetally modelled on yours and feeding
on the corpuscles of
your life's unlearning until
they flutter out and about

the end is always nigh

the Stone Age ended

not because we ran out of stone

what do they know about love what do they know about love what do they know about love what do they know about love what do they know about love what do they know about love what do they know about what do they know about what do they know about what do they know about AssassinationAttackDom esticsecurityDrillExerciseCopsLawenforcementAuthoritiesDisasterassistanc eDisastermanagementDNDO(DomesticNuclearDetectionOffice)Nationalpr eparednessMitigationPreventionResponseRecoveryDirtybombDomesticnucl eardetectionEmergencymanagementEmergencyresponseFirstresponderHom elandsecurityMaritimedomainawareness(MDA)Nationalpreparednessinitiat iveMilitiaShootingShotsfiredEvacuationDeathsHostageExplosion(explosive) PoliceDisastermedicalassistanceteam(DMAT)OrganizedcrimeGangsNationa lsecurityStateofemergencySecurityBreachThreatStandoffSWATScreeningLoc kdownBomb(squadorthreat)CrashLootingRiotEmergencyLandingPipebomb IncidentFacilityHazmatNuclearChemicalspillSuspiciouspackage/deviceToxic NationallaboratoryNuclearfacilityNuclearhreatCloudPlumeRadiationRadioa ctiveLeakBiologicalinfection(orevent)ChemicalChemicalburnBiologicalEpid emicHazardousHazardousmaterialincidentIndustrialspillInfectionPowder(w hite)GasSpilloverAnthraxBlisteragentChemicalagentExposureBurnNerveage ntRicinSarinNorthKoreaOutbreakContaminationExposureVirusEvacuation BacteriaRecallEbolaFoodPoisoningFootandMouth(FMD)H5N1AvianFluSal monellaSmallPoxPlagueHumantohumanHumantoAnimalInfluenzaCenterfo rDiseaseControl(CDC)DrugAdministration(FDA)PublicHealthToxicAgroTe rrorTuberculosis(TB)AgricultureListeriaSymptomsMutationResistantAntivi ralWavePandmicInfectionWaterairborneSickSwinePorkStrainQuarantineH1 N1VaccineTamifluNorvoVirusEpidemicViralHemorrhagicFeverE.ColiInfras tructuresecurityAirportAirplane(andderivatives)ChemicalfireCIKR(CriticalI nfrastructure&KeyResources)AMTRAKCollapseComputerinfrastructureCo mmunicationsinfrastructureTelecommunicationsCriticalinfrastructureNatio nalinfrastructureMetroWMATASubwayBARTMARTAPortAuthorityNBIC(NationalBiosurveillanceIntegrationCenter)TransportationsecurityGridPowe rSmartBodyscannerElectricFailureoroutageBlackoutBrownoutPortDockBrid geCancelledDelaysServicedisruptionPowerlinesDrugcartelViolenceGangDru gNarcoticsCocaineMarijuanaHeroinBorderMexicoCartelSouthwestJuarezSin aloaTijuanaTorreonYumaTucsonDecapitatedU.S.ConsulateConsularElPasoF ortHancockSanDiegoCiudadJuarezNogalesSonoraColombiaMarasalvatrucha MS13orMS13DrugwarMexicanarmyMethamphetamineCarteldeGolfoGulfC artelLaFamiliaReynosaNuevoLeonNarcosNarcobanners(Spanishequivalents) LosZetasShootoutExecutionGunfightTraffickingKidnapCalderonReyosaBus tTamaulipasMethLabDrugtradeIllegalimmigrantsSmuggling(smugglers)Mat amorosMichoacanaGuzmanArellanoFelixBeltranLeyvaBarrioAztecaArtistic AssassinsMexiclesNewFederationTerrorismAlQaeda(allspellings)TerrorAtta ckIraqAfghanistanIranPakistanAgroEnvironmentalterroristEcoterrorismCo nventionalweaponTargetWeaponsgradeDirtybombEnrichedNuclearChemic alweaponBiologicalweaponAmmoniumnitrateImprovisedexplosivedeviceIE

D(ImprovisedExplosiveDevice)AbuSayyafHamasFARC(ArmedRevolutionar
yForcesColombia)IRA(IrishRepublicanArmy)ETA(EuskaditaAskatasuna)Ba
squeSeparatistsHezbollahTamilTigersPLF(PalestineLiberationFront)PLO(Pa
lestineLiberationOrganizationCarbombJihadTalibanWeaponscacheSuicideb
omberSuicideattackSuspicioussubstanceAQAP(ALQaedaArabianPeninsula)
AQIM(AlQaedaintheIslamicMaghreb)TTP(TehrikiTalibanPakistan)YemenPi
ratesExtremismSomaliaNigeriaRadicalsAlShabaabHomegrownPlotNationalis
tRecruitmentFundamentalismIslamistEmergencyHurricaneTornadoTwisterT
sunamiEarthquakeTremorFloodStormCrestTemblorExtremeweatherForestfi
reBrushfireIceStranded/StuckHelpHailWildfireTsunamiWarningCenterMagn
itudeAvalancheTyphoonShelterinplaceDisasterSnowBlizzardSleetMudslideor
MudslideErosionPoweroutageBrownoutWarningWatchLighteningAidReliefC
losureInterstateBurstEmergencyBroadcastSystemCybersecurityBotnetDDOS
(dedicateddenialofservice)DenialofserviceMalwareVirusTrojanKeyloggerCyb
erCommand2600SpammerPhishingRootkitPhreakingCainandabelBruteforci
ngMysqlinjectionCyberattackCyberterrorHackerChinaConfickerWormScam
mersSocialmediawhatdotheyknowaboutlovewhatdotheyknowaboutlovewhatdothey
knowaboutlovewhatdotheyknowaboutlovewhatdotheyknow

is this thing on?

pattern recognition
pushing the envelope

is that a tiger in the long grass?
type II error in cognition
false negative
you're lunch
        the word made flesh

Never get out of the boat.

Absolutely goddamn right!
Unless you were goin' all the way ...

and i
('ox mute') mutus superintendent
spake unto

words
signal and noise
fractured transmissions
settling Cantor dust
a manifesto of inverse recursion

the end is always nigh

things f a l l a p a r t ; t h e c e n t r e
c a n n o t h o l d ;

whATDOTheYkNoWaBoUtLOvEwhATDotHEYkNowAboUtloVewHAtdotheyKNo waboutLOve01110111 01101000 01100001 01110100 00100000 01100100 01101111 00100000 01110100 01101000 01100101 01111001 00100000 01101011 01101110 01101111 01110111 00100000 01100001 01100010 01101111 getting between a ghost and its food has its consequences—as any kid who's been warned will tell you 01110101 01110100 00100000 01101100 01101111 01110110 01100101 00001010 01110111 01101000 01100001 01110100 00100000 01100100 01101111 00100000 01110100 01101000 lo⊠⊠ ⊠qon⊠ ⊠uo⊠ ⊠⊠⊠⊠ po ⊠⊠⊠⊠ 01100101 01111001 00100000 01101011 01101110 01101111 01110111 00100000 01100001 01100010 01101111 01110101 01110100 00100000 01101100 And we could dance. Dance, dance, dance, dance, dance, to the radio. Dance, dance, dance, dance, dance, to the radio. Dance the tarantella. Shake your tail-feather. Lose yourself. Dance, dance, dance, dance, dance, to the radio. Dance, dance, dance, dance, dance, to the radio. under his feet, Shiva crushes the demon of ignorance 01101111 01110110 01100101 00001010 01110111 01101000 01100001 01110100 00100000 01100100 01101111 00100000 01110100 01101000 01100101 01111001 00100000 01101011 01101110 01101111 01110111 00100000 01100001 01100010 01101111 01110101 01110100 00100000 01101100 01101111 01110110 01100101 01101111 01110110 01100101 00001010 01110111 01101000 01100001 01110100 00100000 01100100 01101111 00100000 01110100 01101000 01100101 01111001 00100000 01101011 01101110 01101111 01110111 00100000 01100001 01100010 01101111 01110101 01110100 00100000 01101100 01101111 01110110 0110010101110100 00100000 01101100 00001010 01110111 01101000 01100001 01110100 00100000 01100100 01101111 00100000 01110100 01101000 01100101 01111001 00100000 01101011 01101110 01101111 01110111 00100000 01100001 01100010 01101111 01110101 01110100 00100000 01101100 01101111 01110110 01100101 01101111 01110110 01100101 00001010 01110111 01101000 01100001 01110100 00100000 01100100 01101111 00100000 01110100 01101000 01100101 01111001 00100000 01101011 01101110 01101111 01110111

00100000 01100001 01100010 01101111

(1) $\Delta q \times \Delta v > \hbar/m$
(2) there ain't no captain / in this sinking ship of fools
(3) my mouth is full of dirt, my mouth is full of dirt!
(4) $C = 2B \operatorname{Log}_2 \{(1 + {}^{S}/_{N})^{1/2}\} = B \operatorname{Log}_2 \{1 + {}^{S}/_{N}\}$
(5) barking at the full worm moon

  things fall apart; the centre
cannot hold;

. . . _ _ _ . . .

we understand reflex induced firing or externally induced firing ... but spontaneous firing remains uncertain

axons and dendrites
synaptic clefts

a dark homunculus
running circles
in a faulty hamster-wheel

(sorry, the parenthetic fallacy is filling the hermeneutic gap)

take a drink by the drink

take a dip, in that
 blue lacuna of learning

if it failed it would not return any useful information about the cause of failure if it failed it would not return any useful information about the cause of failure if it failed it would not return any useful information about the cause of failure if it failed it would not return any useful information about the cause of failure if it failed it would not return any useful information about the cause of failure if it failed it would not return any useful information about the cause of failure if it failed it would not return any useful information about the cause of failure if it failed it would not return any useful information about the cause of failure if it failed it would not return any useful information about the cause of failure

vitoð ér enn, eða hvat?

if an eavesdropper attempts to read out the message in transit, they will be discovered by the disturbance their measurement causes to the particles as an inevitable consequence

waiting in line for Ragnarök
strapped to the belly of a Möbius strip
he fills his head with culture
he gives himself an ulcer

nobody
        likes a tourist

and still
i can't find the right words
when
i look at her

she's 50 ft of signal
and i'm just pissing in the wind
my back up against a wall of noise

watching
a serpent eating its own tail

                        in the beginning,

something about the word.

Sources (an incomplete list)

- Christine Brooke-Rose from the book *THRU*
- Guillermo del Toro from online article at http://www.newyorker.com/reporting/2011/02/07/110207fa_fact_zalewski?currentPage=all
- Online article at http://ourgodisspeed.blogspot.com.au/2011/12/lineage-way-of-all-flesh.html
- Anti-entartete Gestapo regulations for playing jazz, circa WWII Nazi-occupied Czechoslovakia
- *Statements on Appropriation* by Michalis Pichler
- The song *Seasick* by The Jesus Lizard
- *Reading the Graphic Surface: The Presense of the Book in Prose Fiction* By Glyn White
- The song *Mask* by Iggy Pop
- Virgil's description of Charon from the Sixth Book Of *The Aeneis*
- The song *I Wanna Be Your Dog* by The Stooges
- Some kid called Billy, found online but I have no idea from where at this point
- From an online source (unknown) about Dante's inferno
- The song *End of Radio* by Shellac
- Sigils used to summon a common demon of hell – from an online source (unkown)
- Sigil for the demon Hamaliel, lord of obsessions – from an online source (unkown)
- Jim Jarmusch – not sure of original source, I found the quote online
- The song *Walk On The Wild Side* by Lou Reed
- Online reference about what goes on in the brain during an episode of cognitive dissonasance
- *Tractatus Logico-Philosophicus* by Ludwig Wittgenstein (Pears/McGuinness translation)
- http://infranetlab.org/blog/islands-waste-1
- Roland Barthes from *Death of the Author*
- The song *I Closed My Eyes And A Truck Came Through The Window* by The Dumb Earth
- The song *Jingle Of A Dog's Collar* by Butthole Surfers
- The song *Say Goodbye* by Hunters and Collectors
- The song *Exit Everything* by Roland S Howard
- Brion Gysin – source unknown
- Peggy Nelson – unkown online source
- The song *Search and Destroy* by Iggy and The Stooges
- Pierre Comeille's *Le Cid*
- Julia Kristeva – source unkown
- The film *Nostalghia* (dir. Andrei Tarovsky)

- The song *Hallelujah* by Leonard Cohen
- The song *There Stands The Glass* written by Russ Hull, Mary Jean Shurtz and Audrey Greisham
- The song *Black Coffee* by Black Flag
- The song *Gray Goes Black* by Mark Lannegan
- *DSM-V*, American Psychiatric Association
- *The Bible* (King James version)
- The song *Rose-Coloured Windscreen* by Kim Salmon
- The Lester Dent Pulp Master Plot
- *Second Coming* by William Butler Yeats
- The song *A Light So Dim* by The Black Heart Procession
- The song *Bad, Bad World* by Firewater
- *Department of Homeland Security National Operations Center Media Monitoring Capability Desktop Reference Binder* 2011
- The film *Apocalypse Now (dir. Francis Ford Coppola)*
- The song *Transmission* by Joy Division
- The song *Ship of Fools* by American Speedway
- *Poetic Edda* poem *Völuspá*, stanza 41
- The song *At Home He's A Tourist* by Gang of Four
- Various Wikipedia pages
- Other long-forgotten sources

www.ingramcontent.com/pod-product-compliance
Lightning Source LLC
Chambersburg PA
CBHW021117080526
44587CB00010B/555
* 9 7 8 1 8 7 6 5 0 2 1 9 5 *